GOD VS SCIENCE

ITS NOT A WAR

SANDIP KUMAR NAYAK

This book does not trying to creat any violence. Its all are just my thoughts. I don't want to influence anyone. If you believe in GOD then believe I don't have any issue, but then you shouldnot force any person to believe your thought.

Contents

Preface

God created the whole universe, he doesn't need our protection.

Religion is a mindset to bring people together but with their consent, not forcefully.

Acknowledgements

The pics I used in this book are derived from random internet searching.

CHAPTER ONE

GOD VS SCIENCE

It has been a long fight continuing between two groups. One of these group are believing in God, but some people are denying that there is no God.

From the time human started socializing they believe in different Gods. At the beginning society created a term "Dharma" which means Religion. This is what history of human told us, but our ancestors told us that God created us. That's the reason behind all the debate and confusion.

Look I am not saying God doesn't exist, but I believe God is not a Physical thing. We can find God in everything we want to see. Science is also agreed that there is a source of energy that controls our mind to think.

As per our ancient books (Veda,purana and Upanisadas) we can find so much information about Gods and their powers and abilities. In the childhood we heard them from our Grandparent and now we can read them too. There are so many proof found at so many places all over the world. Specially proofs from the Hindu religion.

Except Hinduism there are so many religions in the world. Like Muslim,Christian,Sikh,Baudh,Jain etc. But we will talk about Hinduism, because I don't know much about other religion, their culture and believe. The second reason is I am a Hindu.

CHAPTER TWO

What is Dharma ?

As per my understanding religion or Dharma is believe, it basically decide the way of living. So it became very simple to understand that it means what we believe is my Dharma. So as per believe, we made some rule and we followed those rules to be in our dharma or to protect our religion. But there is a misunderstanding how can we protect our God who created us? God has supreme power so they don't need any protection. They protect us in every situation. So we don't have that much power to protect them. What we are doing is? We are protecting their reputation from the people who try to destroy it. But sometimes it pays some price.

<u>What is the Hinduism?</u>

Hinduism believes that every human on the surface of earth is the creation of Lord Brahma. Lord Vishnu is the guardian and Lord Shiva is the destructor. These are the three supreme God of Hinduism.

Besides the three supreme God there are also 33 koti Devata in Hinduism. Koti means type not Cr.

Hinduism allows us to worship everything. We worship sun, fire, wind, water, Mountain, Cow, tree almost everything. Non-Hindu person can say this is madness but it's nothing like that. Worshiping everything results to bring respect and concern towards those things. Like save the trees and animals from killing. But now these days Hindu not following own rule. Actually it's human nature. We change the rule which not helping us. Like we need to build house then we can cut some trees and we can worship other trees. We can't kill animals but we want to eat meat, so some animals can be killed. Hinduism clearly says eating meat is a sin. But we eat because we like it.

Hinduism says respect women, but so many Hindu families killed their female fetus because they want boy child. I am not saying all Hindus doing that but some are doing these sin. So it hurts and we feel ashamed by saying that we are Hindu.

CHAPTER THREE

From where it started?

So as per our ancestors, when universe was not created there was a energy which divided into three parts. The three parts converted in to three supreme entities called as Brahma, Vishnu and Shiva.

THE TRINITY

The energy source assigned them to their work. Lord Brahma assigned for creation

Lord Brahma

, Lord Vishnu assigned to guide the creation to be better

Lord Vishnu

and Lord Shiva assigned to destroy all to restart the universe.

Lord Shiva

They were also has their own residence. Lord Brahma lives in "Brahmalok", lord Vishnu lives in "Vaikunth" and Lord Shiva lives in "Kailash".

All these entities also has their own personality. Lord Brahma is looks like a sage with beard and he has four heads. Lord Vishnu is looks like a king with calm and pleasing nature. He always has a smile on his face. Lord Shiva was not very fond of ornaments and also doesn't care about look. He always sat on meditation.

The three supreme entities has their partners. Lord Brahma has Devi Saraswati, Lord Vishnu has Devi Laxmi and Lord Shiva has Devi Parvati.

Devi Laxmi

Devi Durga

Devi Saraswati

Among the three entities only Lord Shiva has Children. The children of Lord Shiva are also Gods. Lord Ganesha is the God of knowledge and Lord Kartika is the God of war.

As per the assigned work Lord Brahma started to build the earth. First he create essential materials like water, fire, land, food resources etc. After building the materials he created the first human, who called as Manu.

Maharshi Manu

As we all burned from Manu we all called as "Manava".

So as per our ancient sculpture this is how the life on earth started.

science says about

<u>**So what science says about the start of life on earth?**</u>

As per our scientists the universe was started from a big bang. Two supreme energy sources clashed with each other and our planet was formed.

First the temperature of surface of earth was very high. The surface was full of Lava. Then after some million or billion years it began to lose its temperature. The surface now filled with water. There was water everywhere.

In that water our first life form was developed and that is called as amoeba or unicellular organism.

Then cell division process took place and then from unicellular organism to multi-cellular organism we all evaluated gradually. So there was no God who created us. This statement raises a question. What was that force who caused the Big bang? Science yet never explained that and it is always a guess. So as per science the thing we can't explain is not truth. That's where science is looks not confident.

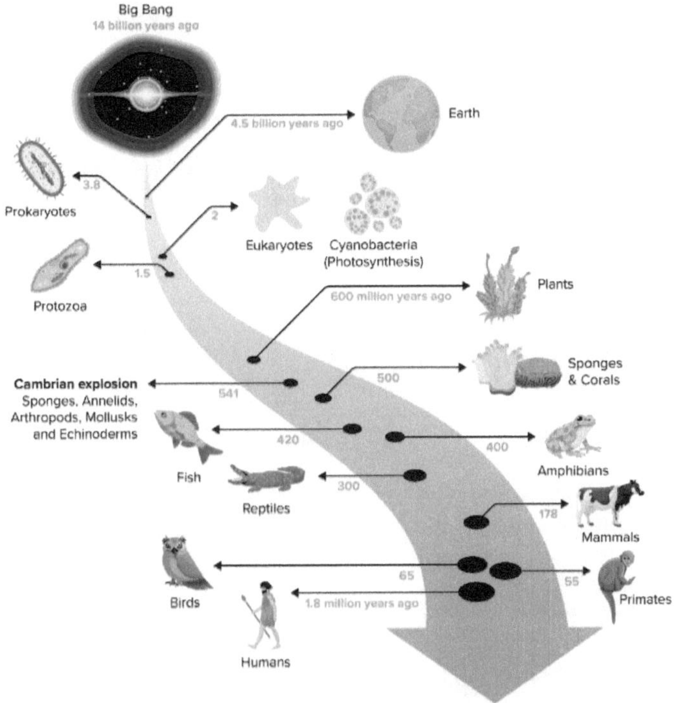

Life formation onn earth

Look I am not saying God power exists but some scientists believes in God.

Like some theories of science has also derived from our ancient sculptures like Bhagwat Gita and Mahabharat.

Science proven that we are living on an oval planet. Science shows there are other planets around our planet. Science shows the picture of our universe.

Science brings us some facility to make our life easier. Science made us confident to do something by own.

Science gives eyes to see outside of our world. But we have to admit that the ancient sculptures are scientifically true.

CHAPTER FIVE

Superstitions and Myths

<u>Superstitions and Myths</u>

This is the part where we have to see what is right or what is wrong for us, because there is a thin line between believe and superstition.

As per the ancient sculptures...

God created us, this is believe but we have to protect God this is superstition. God is not a physical thing and has enough power to protect themselves.

We are just the creation of God. We were created by them to worship them not to protect them.

Long time ago there were some shameful rituals were performed to protect the religion or God. We use to sacrifice small sheep or goat or some other animals. Is this Hinduism? No, because Hinduism teaches us to remove violence and anger. So how we can say Hinduism believes correct?

Who gave us the right to take the life of other animal?

So these type of rituals are not part of Hinduism.

Hinduism teaches us we must avoid 6 enemies and they are related to our behavior.

Six enemies

As per our ancient sculptures we must avoid the six enemies. The six enemies are kama(lust),krodha(anger), Lobha(Greed), Moha(inflatuation), Mada(Arrogance) and Matsara(jealousy).

Kama(Lust)

We must avoid lust, because it takes us towards a wrong mindset. It affects our social life and thinking towards humanity.

Krodha(Anger)

Anger is an emotion which can easily stop our brain to think positive. So we must avoid anger.

Lobha(Greed)

Greed is not gives any profit to our life. When we became greedy then we stops thinking about others. So in the end we lost everyone.

Moha(Infatuation)

Infatuation for anything makes us blind minded that we can't even think what is right or wrong.

Mada(Arrogance)

Arrogance is not good for us because it destroys our true personality. Nothing is truly made only for us. So why should we show arrogance.

Matsara(Jealousy)

Everyone in the world working so hard for their achievements, so there is no profit in jealousy. What we got it's the result of our hard work and dedication. If we fail somewhere then it may be lack of focus. So there is no point to be jealous.

SO these are the six enemies mentioned is our Hindu mythologics.

But no one is following these words properly.

This proves of misunderstanding of Mythology or Veda or Puranas.

Not only Hindu other religions are also misunderstanding their mythology.

For example, In Islam there are 41 times mentioned in Quran about Jihad. It means try to awaken the truth of Islam to its pure form.

But they only understood that killing of kafirs.

As per Quran a kafir means, "Who declines to accept the truth of Allah." It doesn't mentioned Hindu only, but Jihadis understood kafir means only Hindu.

So these wrong understanding of Veda and mythology leads us towards some superstitions.

People who believes in science, fights with religious people because of these superstitions.

Because these superstitions killed so many people.

There are so many religions in the world but only two religions are violent in nature, which their religious books not said to do. Hence it means they don't believe their own religions. They are trying to protect their religions, which is a foolish thought. As per the sculptures and Vedas religions are decided as per the lifestyle they are living or as per the believes. We can't force someone believe what we believe. Every individual has their own mindset so he is free to believe what he wants to believe.

This is where Science came.

Science told us to believe what we have seen. Science tells us to believe the physical presence of a matter.

For example we saw sun rises in east then we believe it. Science says Mangal, Sun, Moon, Jupitor, and Saturn are planets and these are space matters.

Some people say they do have a impact for the lives on earth.

It is true but that nothing to do with our lifestyle. Ultraviolet ray helps trees for photosynthesis that does not contain any purity or impurity.

There is a debate going on in an Indian state Odisha that whether it is necessary to take cooked food during solar eclipse or not.

solar eclipse

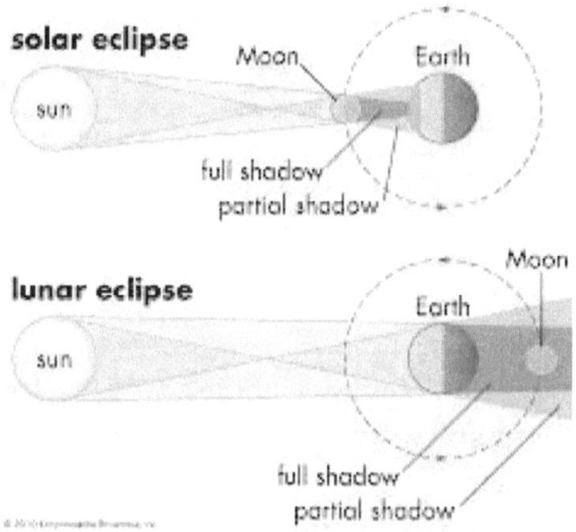

I would say it's not necessary to take food but it also not mandatory to leave cooking.

It's a culture of Hindu religion. But there is nothing to do with impact of Sun.

If some people don't want to follow the culture then we can't force them to do so. But there is nothing bad to follow the tradition if it is not harmful to our society.

Leave cooking during solar eclipse is not harmful for society. Hence we can follow the tradition but if someone wanted to eat cooking food we can't force him to not eat. It's a personal choice and every person has his right to make his own choice.

CHAPTER SEVEN

My opinion

So honestly I don't mind whether God exists or not. I believe in humanity. I will stand against the rules if it is harmful to anybody.

God might be a myth, it might not exists in real world but people believes in it, that's what matters. Yes, there are some rituals which are not safe for living organisms; we should stand against those foolish rituals.

When we have doubt in our mind for something we don't understand we are following our internal feeling. That what God is, it's the trust that we have in our mind about certain things.

We trust on us for doing something we never did before, that trust is God.

If a person is trouble and if we can help him then we became God to that person.

I can say we are just reading books not learning from it.

Our Holy books contains so many nice things what we can learn from it, but we only choose the wrong meaning of them.

Our holy book says, "Basudhaiba kutumbakam." It means, "The whole world is our family." But some people say Hindus are great, some says Muslims are great, some

says Christians are great.
I will say Humanity is the best religion in the world.

Thoughts

"Trust on God but not blindly follow the religion."

"God created the whole universe, he doesn't need our protection."

"Religion is a mindsct to bring people together but with their consent, not forcefully."

"Science can't explain the supreme power what religious people called God, it doesn't mean that they should stop believing on God."

We can't say wrong to science or religion because both are so separate to each other and both are necessary to our life.

With religion we got confidence and with science we can find the truth behind every miracle.

I will suggest not to fight with each other, until science finds the truth behind our mythology.